This book belongs to:

____

First & second Grade workbook

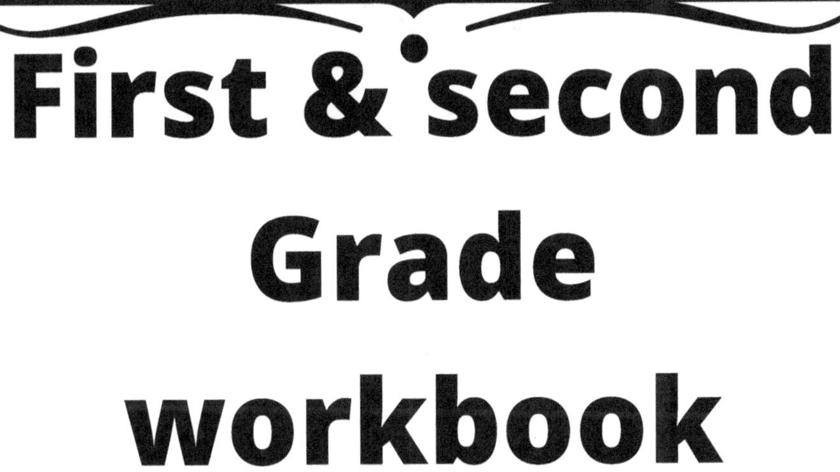

Mathematics

Grammar

Reading

Coloring

Writing

Jack Brown

Grade 1

<u>Jumping Math</u>

1.
5 + 3 =

2.
1 + 8 =

3.
1 + 3 =

4.
1 + 4 =

5.
5 + 4 =

6.
6 + 3 =

7.
3 + 6 =

8.
2 + 3 =

9.
3 + 2 =

Start addition

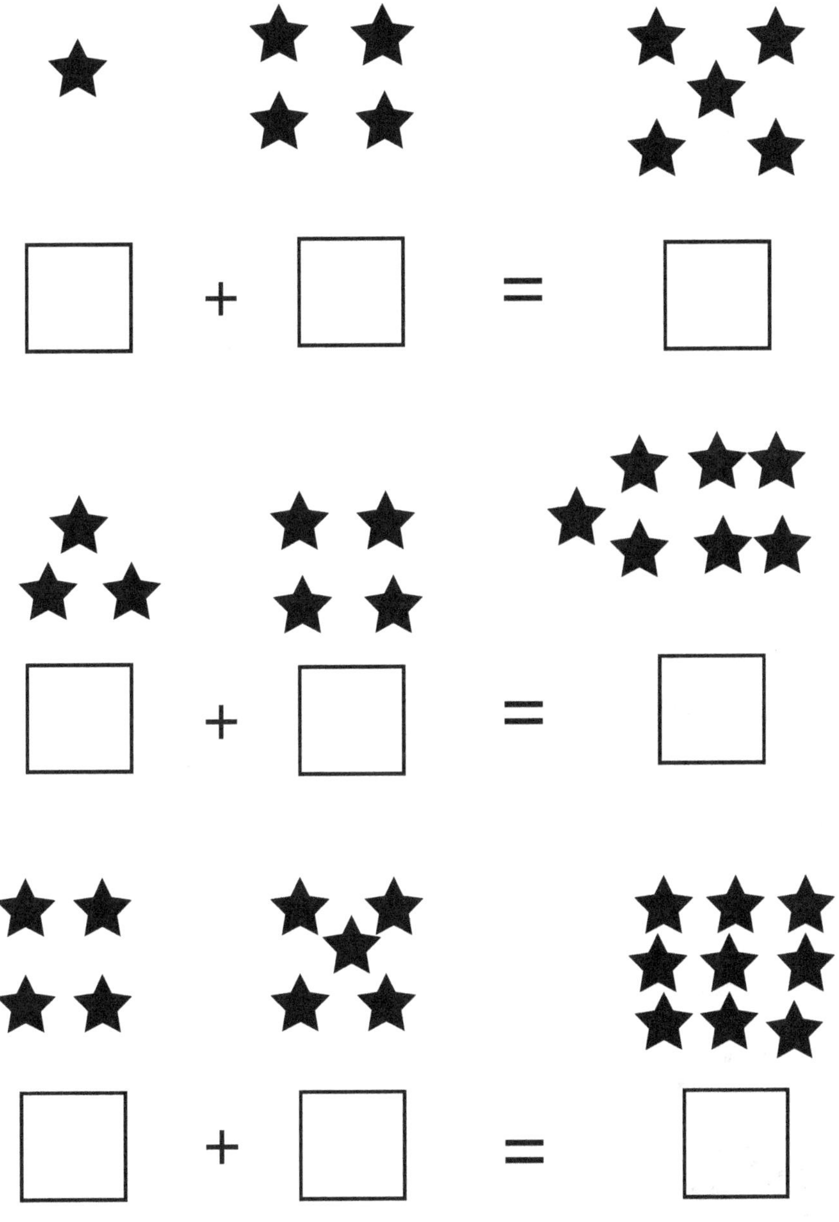

Beginning blends

Common Sight Words

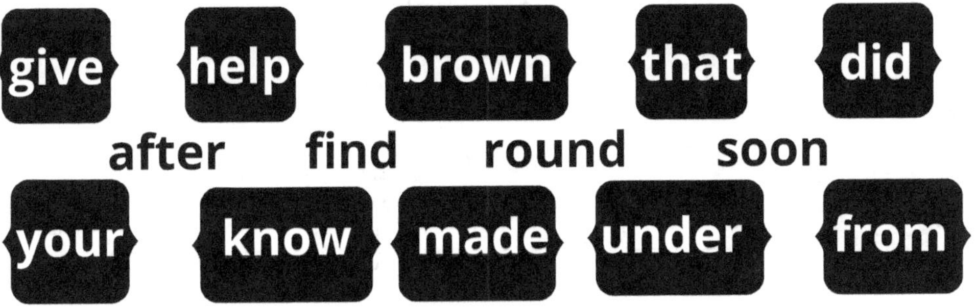

1_Is that _______favorite book?

2_ I got a cookie _______the store.

3_The dog has_________fur.

4_I like to _______cook dinner.

5_I __________yummy snack.

6_Did you _______my red hat?

7_My shoes are ________the bed.

 _____ock

 _____ower

 _____oves

 _____ag

 _____mp

 App_____

 _____on

 ___ps

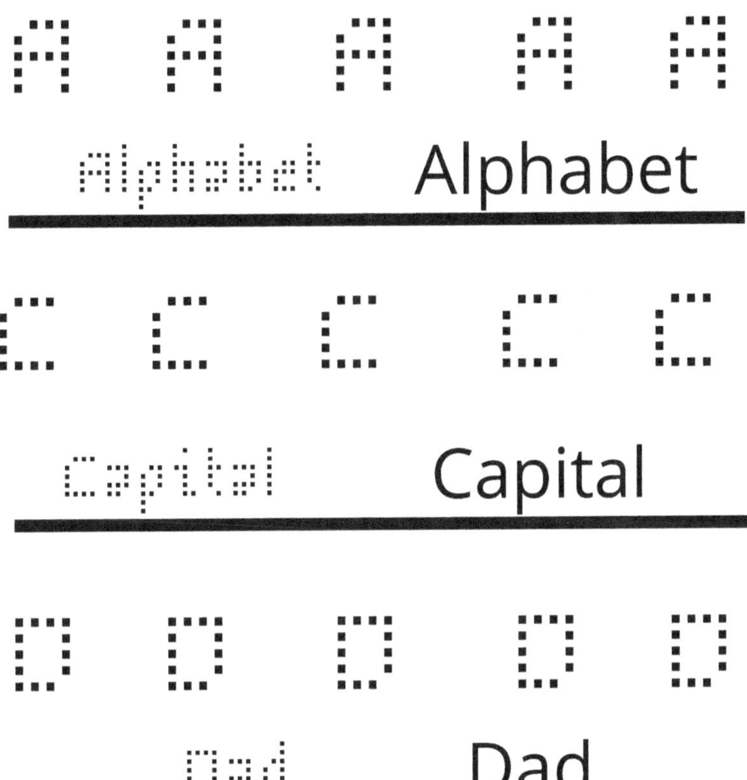

Alphabet

Capital

Dad

Colored By:

1		3	4	5		7		9	10
11		13		15	16	17		19	
21	22		24	25	26		28	29	30
31	32	33	34	35	36	37	38	39	
	42		44		46	47	48	49	50
51	52	53	54	55	56		58	59	60
61		63		65		67	68	69	
71	72		74	75	76			79	80
	82	83	84		86	87	88		90
91	92		94	95		97	98		100

Letter Recognition

T   e   w   t   h
☐ ☐ ☐ ☐

A   m   a   g   n
☐ ☐ ☐ ☐

Q   q   f   r   i
☐ ☐ ☐ ☐

L   d   o   l   a
☐ ☐ ☐ ☐

P   u   t   p   c
☐ ☐ ☐ ☐

Nouns and Verbs

Use this nouns and verbs to complete the sentences below, **each word used only once.**

Bake   eat   cake   made   pie

Verb

1_I like to_ _ _ _ _ _ _ _ cookies with my family.

2_My dad likes biscuit best, but my mum's

Noun

favourite is pumpkin_ _ _ _ _ _ _ _ _. _.

Verb

3_My sister_ _ _ _ _ _ _ dessert fast than I do.

Noun

4_I helped bake my own birthday_ _ _ _ _ _ _.

5_Cupcakes for my friend's birthday party

Verb

_ _ _ _ _ _ .

Add or Substract The Numbers

10 - 7 = ☐ **W**

3 + 7 = ☐ **O**

6 + 2 = ☐ **S**

9 - 5 = ☐ **N**

1 + 1 = ☐ **A**

5 + 4 = ☐ **M**

write the letters that go with the numbers
in the boxes to find out !

8	4	10	3	9	2	4

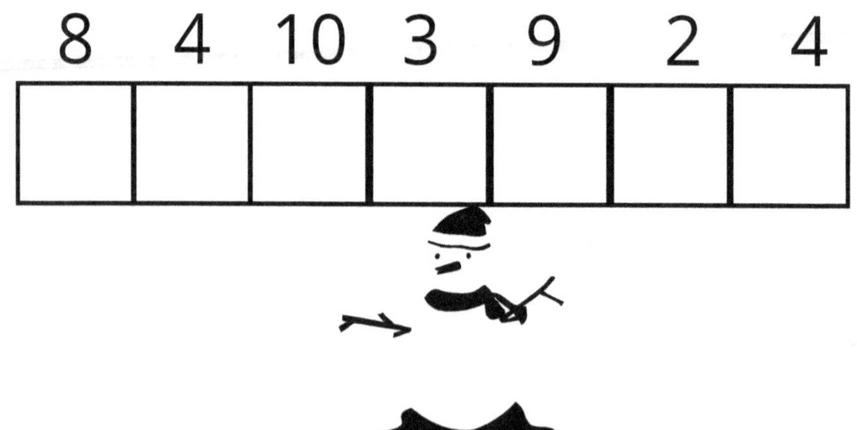

Learn to Tell Time

12:20 ☐

11:00 ☐

4:00 ☐

6:40 ☐

8:30 ☐

8:05 ☐

4:05 ☐

3:03 ☐

12:16 ☐

12:20 ☐

11:00 ☐

4:20 ☐

Writing time 2

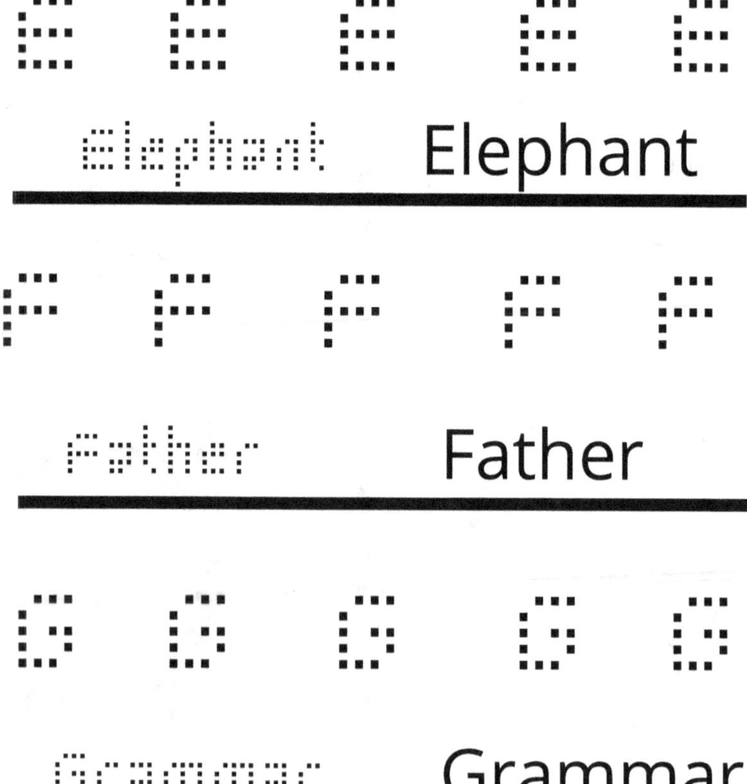

elephant Elephant

Father Father

Grammar Grammar

Colored By:

____

Missing Numbers   ②

1		3		5		7		9	10
11				15	16			19	
	22		24		26		28	29	30
31	32			35	36	37	38	39	
	42		44		46	47			50
51	52	53	54				58	59	60
61			65		67		69		
	72			75	76			79	80
	82		84		86	87			90
91			94	95			98		100

<u>Parts of a Centences</u>

Draw a line to match each naming part with an action part

Naming Parts

The quick puppy
Anna
The Park
My brother
The cats
Summer

Auction Parts

is coming soon
at all of the snakes
want a new bike
is my favourite place
is going to the zoo
jumped over the log

Start the countdown

10	9	8	7	6		4	3	2	1

20	19	18	17	16		14	13	12	11

10	9		7	6	5	4		2	1

20	19	18		16		14	13	12	11

10	9		7	6		4	3	2	1

Reading Time

one	Color	Hand	Rabbit	Cat
Dog	Three	Leg	Blue	Doll
Girl	Bird		Yellow	Four
Brown	Head	Five	Animal	Toy
Fish	Feet	Red	Two	Black

<u>Creative Writing</u> 

Complete the sentence below

1_My favorite subject in school is____________

____

2_Some of my school supplies are____________

____

3_My best friends at school are____________

____

4_At launch time I like to eat____________

____

5_The name of my school is ____________

____

6_My teacher's name is ____________

____

Hotel

Internet

June

Colored By:

____

1		3		5				9	10
11				15	16			19	
	22		24		26			29	30
	32			35		37	38	39	
	42		44		46	47			50
51		53	54				58		60
61				65		67		69	
	72			75				79	80
	82		84		86	87			90
91				95			98		100

\> < =

35 ☐ 52		40 ☐ 42
30 ☐ 29		16 ☐ 19
74 ☐ 42		36 ☐ 12
97 ☐ 97		12 ☐ 20
20 ☐ 22		87 ☐ 87
78 ☐ 87		36 ☐ 63

Beginning Blends

Fill the blanks with the correct consonant blend

____ar

____oon

____obe

____w

____ane

____or

<u>Fill in the verb</u>

gives   has   know   asks
start   think   walks

1_ Jared_______________many pets.

2_ Mike __________running at 6 am.

3_ Nancy__________ avocado in to 4 pieces to make sandwitches.

4_ I don't_________ what time he would come today.

5_ Mr Hass _________ me for change.

6_ Lisa ___________6 miles to school.

7_ I _______about my dream last night.

Words That Start With Ch

Chap	Char	Chat	Chip	Chow
Champ	Chain	Chair	Chalk	Cheap
Cheat	Check		Cheek	Cheer
Chest	Chick	chief	Child	Chili
Cheese	Chance	Cherry	Chicken	Choco-late

K K K K K

King   **King**

L L L L L

Love   **Love**

---

m m m m m

march   **March**

Colored By:

____

1		3		5				9	10
11				15	16			19	
	22		24		26			29	30
	32			35		37		39	
	42		44			47			50
51			54				58		60
61				65		67		69	
	72			75				79	80
	82		84		86	87			90
91				95			98		100

Start the countdown

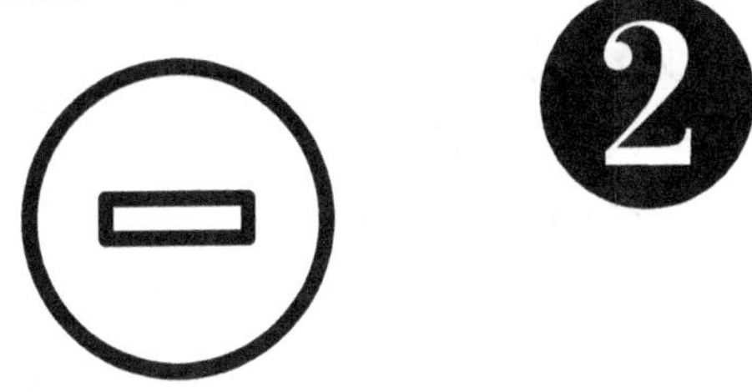

10	9	8	7	6		4	3	2	

20	19	18	17	16		14	13	12	11

10	9		7	6	5	4			1

20	19	18		16		14	13		11

30	29	28	27	26	25	24	23		20

_______awberry

_______irrel

_______eet

_______ee

_______es

_______lding

American Symbols

```
L A O F A D K S S B J
A P A E L V A T D A A
I L E A F A H A J M S
A I B G G E G R B E F
J B N L H A I S E R U
E E R E S N O U R I N
P R E S I D E N T C E
O T Y A O T Y I I A S
U Y S T R I P E S A T
T S T A T E S N D Z H
```

America   Flag   Liberty

States   President   Eagle

Stripes   Stars

<u>Tell a Silly Animal Tale</u>

Fill the blank with the type of word described

There once was a ___________________
describing word

_____________ from ______________.
Aniimal   Country

Nobody knew he was a______________
Same animal

 because he had _____________ fur and
Color

ate ____________ ____________ each day.
Number   Plural food

He liked to _____________ and sing
action word

______________. Whenever he was
song

_____________ he would start
feeling

speaking__________
Language

Writing time

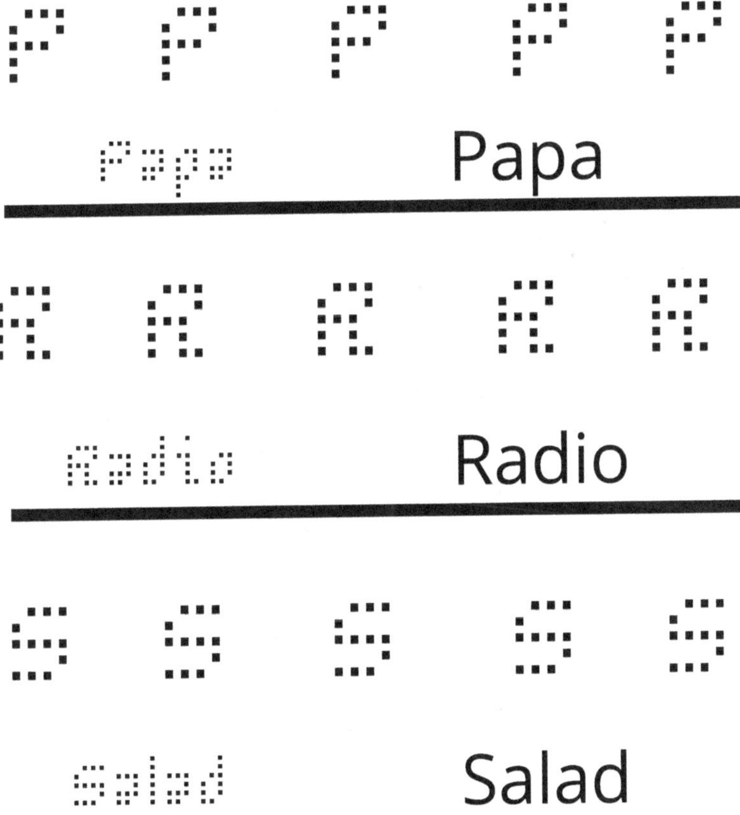

Colored By:

____

<u>Missing Numbers</u> ⬤ **5**

1				5				9	10
11				15	16			19	
	22		24					29	
	32			35		37		39	
	42		44			47			50
51			54				58		60
				65		67		69	
	72			75				79	
	82		84			87			90
91				95			98		

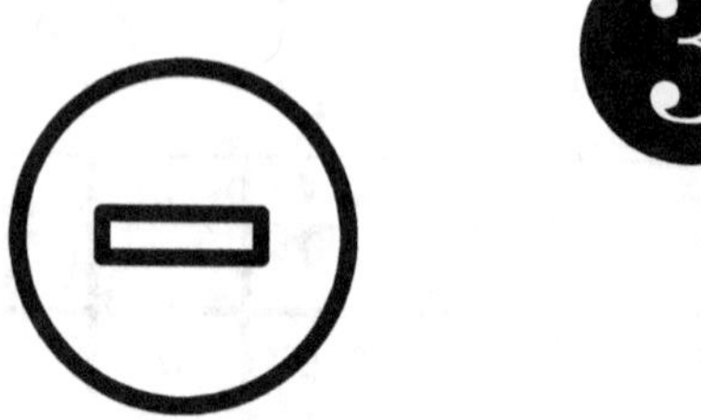

10		8		6		4	3	2	
20		18		16		14		12	11
	9		7			4			1
30	29		27	26		24	23		20
40	39	38	37	36		34	33		31

Ending Blends

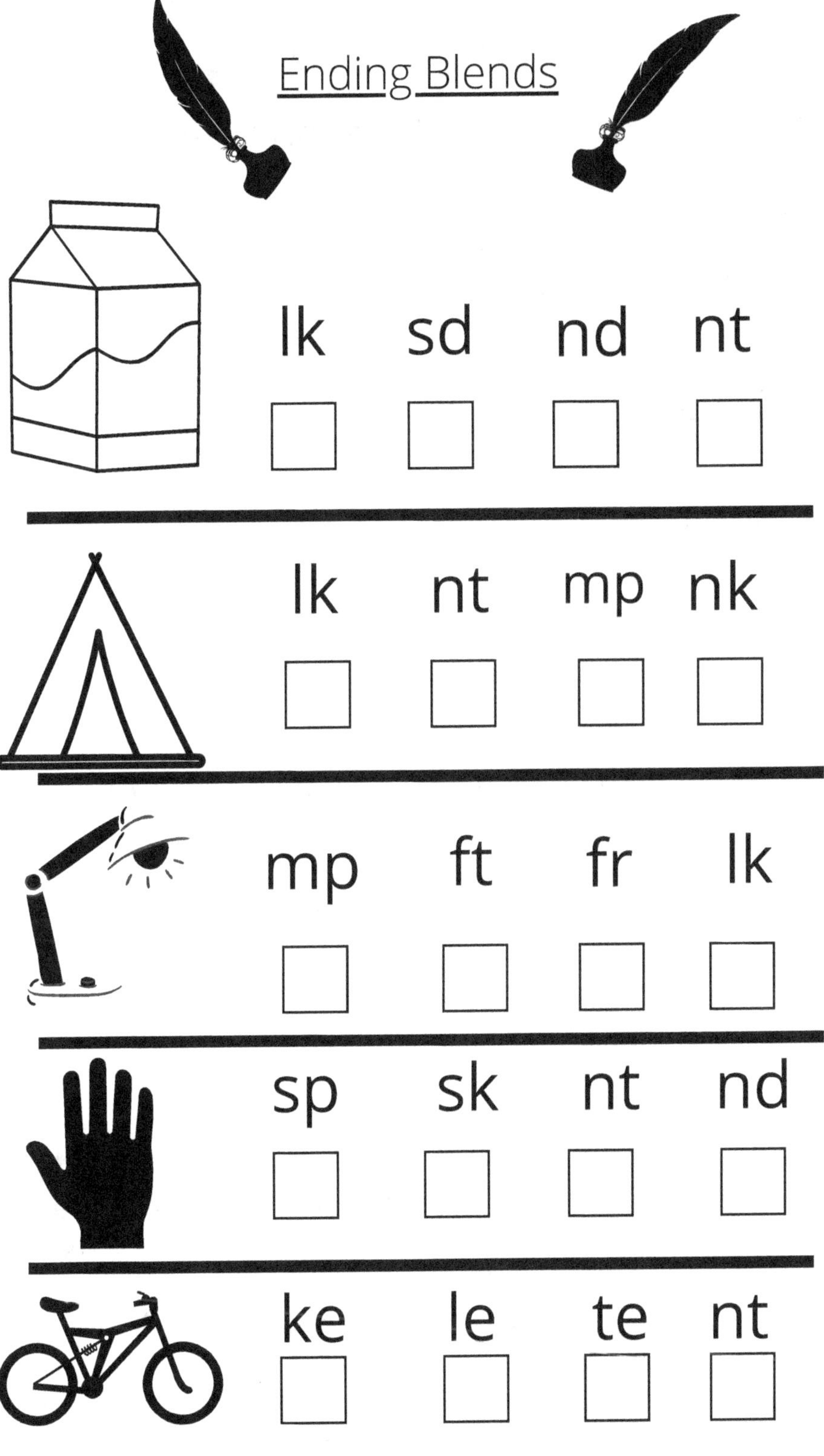

<u>To, Two or Too</u>

To: function word, **Two:** number,
Too: also

1_ I'm going _____ read a book.

2_ Donald Run ______ miles.

3_ Is Ann coming _______?

4_ She got _____ wrong on the test.

5_My brother's like ___ play basketball.

6_I was at the park ______ time today.

7_Those clothes are ______ expensive.

8_ Cinty got _____ strikes in bowling.

9_ I need ___ write ____ pages for school.

<u>Speech Quiz</u>

What kind of word is underlined?

1_ The teacher's <u>shoes</u> are red.
Noun   Adjective   Verb

2_ I always <u>walk</u> to school.
Noun   Adjective   Verb

3_ The <u>cat</u> sleep all day.
Noun   Adjective   Verb

4_ He had <u>green</u> ball.
Noun   Adjective   Verb

5_ Grandma <u>baked</u> cookies.
Noun   Adjective   Verb

6_ The bady <u>drank</u> milk.
Noun   Adjective   Verb

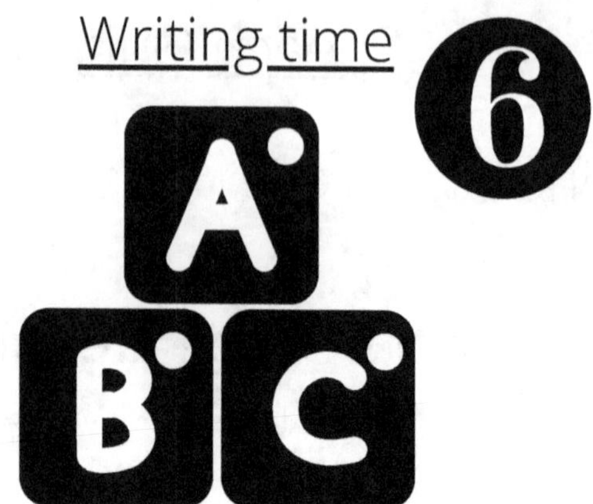

6

T T T T T

Taxi   Taxi

U U U U U

USA   USA

V V V V V

Valid   Valid

Colored By:

____

1				5					10
11					16			19	
	22		24					29	
	32			35				39	
	42					47			50
51			54						60
				65		67		69	
	72							79	
	82					87			90
91				95			98		

Fact families

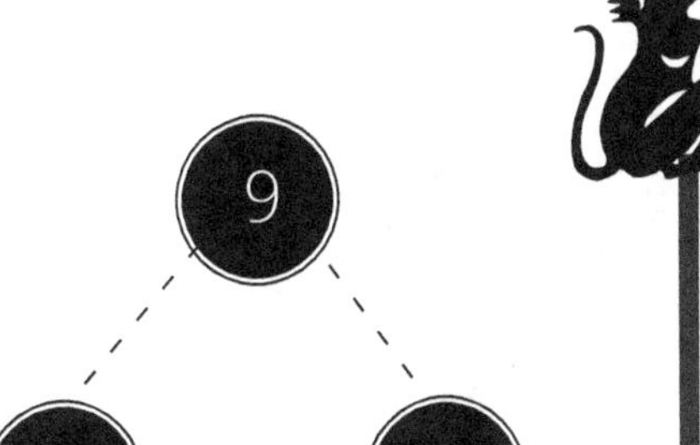

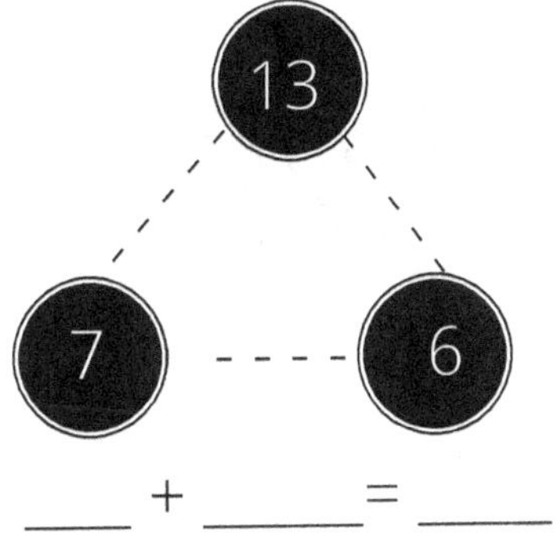

4 + 5 = 9

9 - 5 = 4

___ + ___ = ___

___ - ___ = ___

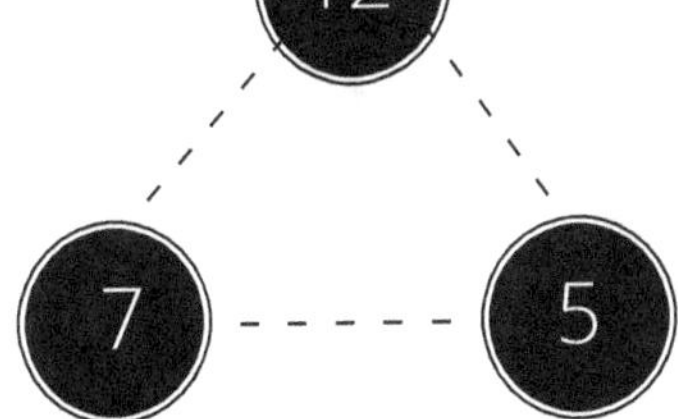

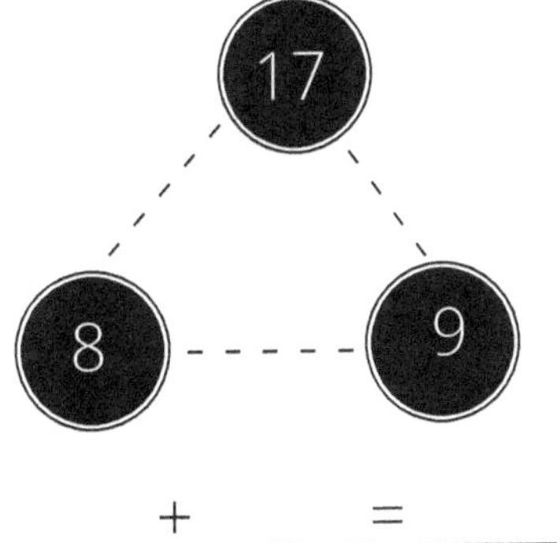

___ + ___ = ___

___ - ___ = ___

___ + ___ = ___

___ - ___ = ___

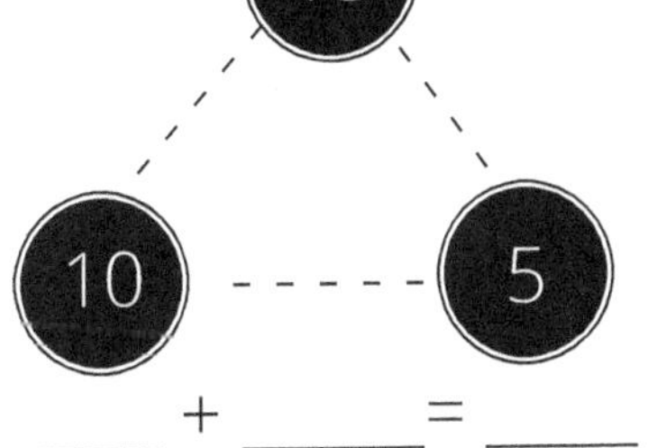

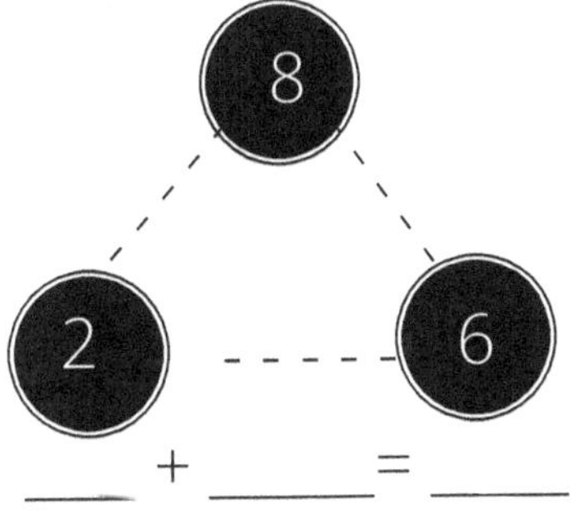

___ + ___ = ___

___ - ___ = ___

___ + ___ = ___

___ - ___ = ___

<u>Read and fill the missing</u>

1_ This _________ 's name is Sam.

2_ He _______ run very fast.

3_ One day he could not found his blue _________.

4_ So He _________ all around town to look for it.

<u>Synonims and Antonyms</u>

Mark the word that has the **same meaning**

make jump ☐ out ☐ world ☐ nail ☐

big little ☐ pickle ☐ elephant ☐ large ☐

yell shoot ☐ brother ☐ tell ☐ whisper ☐

car bike ☐ auto ☐ truck ☐ beer ☐

Mark the word that has the **opposite meaning**

up little ☐ down ☐ over ☐ ugly ☐

small huge ☐ boy ☐ Tony ☐ Hawk ☐

Word

Xavi

You

Colored By:

____